LET GO
OF THE
COOKIES
Do You See What They See In You?

James "J.R." Edwards

LET GO
OF THE
COOKIES

Do You See What They See In You?

JAMES "J.R." EDWARDS

Unless otherwise indicated, all scripture quotations are taken from the King James Version of the Bible.

LET GO OF THE COOKIES

Do You See What They See In You

ISBN: **978-0-578-87838-6**

© 2021 All rights reserved

James "J.R." Edwards

www.BridgetheGapJAE.com

No part of this book may be reproduced or transmitted in any form or by any means, electronic or mechanical, including photocopying, recording, or by any information storage and retrieval system, without permission in writing from the publisher.

DEDICATION

"Let Go Of The Cookies" is dedicated to my wife Keyona Edwards. "Ke" there aren't enough adjectives to describe the depth of love and appreciation I have for you as my best friend and my wife, but I must say that you have been the greatest supporter to me throughout this book writing process and marriage. In 2014 when this book was a thought, you were there encouraging me to pursue it. When we were doing various fundraisers and outreach events you would make sure I hadn't forgotten about writing this book. You have been my motivation and the thoughts that have produced my smiles. I am eternally blessed to be sharing life's odyssey with you by my side. I love you "Stink"!

I would also like to dedicate this book to our children (Kyunnika, Elisha, Lathan, Alex, and Khristina). I want each of you to know that I love you and all things are possible when you acknowledge Christ in all your ways, believe in yourself, stick together, and maintain your integrity in all that you set your heart to do in life.

To my mother Monica Tarpley, you have been my inspiration in so many ways; therefore, I want to document how thankful I am for the many sacrifices you've made so that I could have a good, Godly life. May this book serve as a testament that you did an excellent job as a single mother raising your son. I love you "Ma"!

To my father, grandparents, in-laws, family, friends, and Bridge the Gap Outreach Ministry supporters, thank you for everything you've done and continuously contribute. You are very much loved and appreciated.

To my Pastor, Apostle Lawrence G. Campbell, Sr., thank you for being a father, mentor, advisor, and so much more during the times I needed you to be more than just my pastor. God connected us when I was 19 years old and from there I was blessed to be your organist for over 17 years. Your knowledge, wisdom, and understanding helped to navigate me through many of life's challenges, for which I am grateful. To Mother Gloria,

Elder Larry, Dr. Philip Campbell, and the entire Bible Way Cathedral church family in Danville, Virginia, thank you for all your years of unwavering support. My wife and I are thankful to be members of such a great congregation of believers. We love you all.

In closing, to Bishop George G. Bloomer, thank you for helping to ameliorate my life and for being a man of exceptional integrity. Because of you, I have met African kings, queens, politicians (foreign and domestic), and traveled around the world spreading the good news of the gospel. My wife and I have been greatly enriched holistically through your many impartations. You have made it possible for many goals to be met, from being a part of the White House African American Stakeholders to the purchasing of our first house, and now to the releasing of my first book, you've been an integral part of the process to success. May God continue to strengthen and bless you abundantly.

PREFACE

Growing up in the home of my grandmother, Mable Carter, I can remember that she had a cookie jar in the shape and image of a strawberry sitting on the kitchen table. Often as a youngster, she would allow me to get a cookie from the jar; however, I would try to take out more than one cookie at a time and my hand would get stuck inside of the cookie jar. As I would struggle to remove my hand she would turn and say "If you let go of the cookies, your hand will come out of the jar"! That statement has resonated within me down through the years and has inspired two opposing viewpoints to the thought of "Let Go Of The Cookies"!

First, I considered the viewpoint of the person whose hand is stuck in the cookie jar. Some situations we are in are because we will not let go of the nouns that are preventing us from being released. We find ourselves stuck in frustrating predicaments and get upset when we can't figure a way out.

Then, I thought from the viewpoint of the cookie jar. It has tasteful cookies placed inside of it that need to be released into the life of the person who is reaching for a snack to hold them until they can get a full course meal.

This book is written to serve as that snack to empower, build, strengthen, inspire, and bridge the gap to better ministries, families, communities, friendships, relationships, fellowship, and your self-worth in a holistic way. Ponder these tasteful tidbits as you examine the cookies in your life; even discuss them amongst your peers or in a group study session.
We all have some cookies in our lives whether good or bad that we need to examine, so what cookies are you holding on to?

James "J.R." Edwards

INTRODUCTION

My beloved readers, as we move forward with everyday life, we can't help, but to periodically think about how our daily lives have been impacted due to the outbreak of this pandemic disease called Coronavirus. Despite what we have heard about its effect upon the human body, and how many people have tried to persuade us not to attend church services, there is something on the inside of many of us that said, "If I Can Just Get To The House Of God, I Know I'll Hear A Word From The Lord To Help Me Get Through This!"

One of the perplexities about life is that life has an inconsiderate way of introducing us to "Unexpected Situations" without regard to how those "Un-expectancies" will impact, affect, and alter our lives forever. If I were to take a brief survey today, I believe that everyone would say, "This was unexpected." When life introduces us to an unexpected situation, life simultaneously acquaints us with the age-old question of "Why"? " Why did this have to happen?" "Why Now?" It is when our questions go unanswered that we as human beings begin to panic and do things that we wouldn't normally do to feel comfortable in an uncomfortable circumstance.

I've come to find out that life is filled with many uncomfortable, unexpected situations, and that there will be moments in life where we won't "understand why" certain things had to happen. Those moments in life, I equate to having my hand caught in the cookie jar and if I could just let go of the cookies, I can get free.

As you embark upon this 30-day journey, I encourage you to be completely honest with yourself. This 30-day devotional is broken down into 3 parts: Part 1 "Ships" is dealing with the various relationships we have in our lives, Part 2 "You" is focusing on the things we need to work on within ourselves, and Part 3 "The Plan" deals with how God sees us. After reading each day, take the time to write the things you need to change or release in your life to prepare yourself to Let Go of the Cookies.

James "J.R." Edwards

TABLE CONTENTS

Preface

Introduction................................ ix

Part 1 'Ships'...............................1

Part 2 You...................................37

Part 3 The Plan............................59

James "J.R." Edwards

Part 1
' Ships'

DAY 1
FELLOWSHIP VS RELATIONSHIP

"If we say that we have fellowship with him, and walk in darkness, we lie, and do not the truth:" "But if we walk in the light, as he is in the light, we have fellowship one with another, and the blood of Jesus Christ his Son cleanseth us from all sin."
1 John 1:6-7

Fellowship is the friendly ASSOCIATION with people who share common interests mentally, physically, or spiritually.

Relationship is the CONNECTION of two entities emotionally, physically, or spiritually.

You can have a relationship by being related to a person, but be out of fellowship because of your lack of interaction with that person. A child and their parents have a relationship as a result of being related, but they are not always in fellowship because of their actions in or perception of the relationship.

> **Being honest with yourself starts with acknowledging both the good and bad parts.**

You can have fellowship, but not have a relationship, but you cannot have an effective relationship without an affective fellowship. Many people fellowship with various churches which introduces them to what that ministry is about, but choosing to be in a RELATIONSHIP and CONNECT as a member, gains them access to the rights and privileges that the ministry offers.

We cannot deny that our ASSOCIATIONS and CONNECTIONS are a part of what helps us to adapt to life-changing situations and emerge resiliently. We have to be honest with ourselves, acknowledge both the good and bad parts, admit our own mistakes, learn from them, and move forward.

Today's Prayer:
Lord, please help me to be honest with myself in my 'Ships'.

Today's Reflection

What are some things you have learned about yourself in your 'Ships' that you need to let go of?

DAY 2
JUST BECAUSE IT'S IN THE REFRIGERATOR DOESN'T MEAN YOU HAVE TO TASTE IT

"All things are lawful [that is, morally legitimate, permissible], but not all things are beneficial or advantageous. All things are lawful, but not all things are constructive [to character] and edifying [to spiritual life]."
1 Corinthians 10:23 AMP

Just because you have access to something, doesn't mean you have to partake of it. There are some things that we have access to that God doesn't want us to have. In Genesis Chapter 3, Adam and Eve had access to the tree of the knowledge of good and evil, but God didn't want them to partake of it. In 1st Corinthians 10:23, what Paul is trying to convey is, you have a right to do whatever you choose to do, but what you choose to do, might not be your wisest choice.

> **Don't expect and require something out of others that you aren't willing to require of yourself.**

Your choice doesn't always just affect you, but it can affect your witness to others. Some people look up to you and if they see you do wrong then they feel that it's okay for them also. We all have heard the idiom "*Do as I say and not as I do*", but I say "*Lead by example*". Don't expect and require something out of others that you aren't willing to require of yourself. Just because it's within your reach and in the refrigerator doesn't mean it will edify you.

Today's Prayer:
Lord, give me wisdom and understanding to make the best decisions so that I can lead by example.

Today's Reflection

What are some choices you have to make to help you be the best you?

DAY 3
KEEP YOUR VENT CLOSED

"Whoso keepeth his mouth and his tongue keepeth his soul from troubles."
Proverbs 21:23

Have you ever wondered if you only told one person, how do two, and three other people know about it when they didn't get the information from you? Don't fall for the line of "This conversation is just between you and me".

> **Don't put heavy burdens on weak shoulders!**

It is important to know and establish a person's role in your life. You can't control another person's loyalty. Their actions and how they treat you are a true indicator of the value they place on your friendship. Your best friend may have a best friend and you may not be that best friend to them! You might be venting all your business to your best friend who's venting all their business plus yours to their best friend.

Could what you are about to vent, be more than that person can handle at this time? Is it possible that some of your troubles are a result of you confiding in persons that couldn't bear it? Don't put heavy burdens on weak shoulders! Some conversations should be kept between you and God. Cast all your cares upon God; for he cares for you, and keep your vent closed!

Today's Prayer:
Lord, help me to take an honest spiritual inventory of the friendships I have in my life.

Today's Reflection

Are you talking too much to the wrong people?

DAY 4
WHAT 'SHIPS' ARE YOU HOLDING ON TO?

Fulfill ye my joy, that ye be likeminded, having the same love, being of one accord, of one mind."
Philippians 2:2

God is in this year. He is and will be the same God now and forevermore. This time of quarantine has dramatically impacted the amount of time people spend together. Think it not strange when you hear and see people that you thought would be together for a lifetime start separating and getting divorced, and people who have hung together for years their friendships start ending.

> **It is all a part of the Divine Completeness of God.**

It is all a part of the Divine Completeness of God. The Divine Completeness of God denotes the oneness of the Godhead (Father, Son, and Holy Spirit) in Christ Jesus bringing us (His Children) into alignment with His "good, and acceptable, and perfect, will of God"(Romans 12:2); consequently, causing our spiritual eyes to see those connected to us for who they are.

That friendship or relationship was supposed to end several years ago, but you held on because you thought it was supposed to last a lifetime. It is time for those Relationships and Friendships to be defined for what they are. God is going to spiritually define and show you if the current friendships and relationships are the ones He wants you to be in.

Today's Prayer:
Lord, lead me and guide me to the 'Ships' that you have for me in my life, so I do not hold on to what is not for me.

Today's Reflection

What have you been holding on to that you need to let go of?

DAY 5
ACCEPT WHAT GOD ALLOWS

Let the words of my mouth and the meditation of my heart
Be acceptable in Your sight, O Lord, my rock and my Redeemer.
Psalm 19:14

This year God says "Move on, I have someone better for you." You can't save a marriage, relationship, friendship, or whatever it is you called it, that His hand has already been removed from!! You are fighting a losing battle. This is your scapegoat. You have fought a good fight, but your course is finished. Don't allow your pride to convince you of holding on to that which you should have let go of long before now.

Accept God's answer to your prayers.

If you are not going to accept His answer, regardless of who the messenger is that He uses to send it, then stop praying to Him about the same issues. Just name that relationship 'ICHABOD' which means The Glory Of The Lord Has Left! (1 Samuel 4:21) You have to learn to pray for the peace of the matter, accept God's answer to your prayers, and move on. Move while God's hands are in it!

Today's Prayer:
Lord, I have prayed and you have answered. Please give me the strength to accept what you have ordered for my life and to move on.

Today's Reflection

What are the answers God has given you that you need to learn to accept?

DAY 6
DOES GOD LOVE US?

Herein is love, not that we loved God, but that he loved us, and sent his Son [to be] the propitiation for our sins.
1 John 4:10

As a believer we have to have a solid foundation of fellowship with God to understand His mind and the love He has for us. Getting in God's word is a foundational principle to understand God. Will we ever know everything about God? Unfortunately, the answer is No. Each day that we are in continued fellowship with Him, He will reveal himself and show us His love.

We can understand the mind of God Through The Love of God. The mind of God is vast and multidimensional.

> **He treats us like we never fell from the start.**

He is the same God that knows you are hurt and knows who hurt you. We have to see and know that He chose us before we fell. He knew we would fall, but yet He treats us like we never fell from the start. He sees us in our finished state, Redeemed. The love of God is defined clearly in scripture. It is written, *"For God so loved the world, that He gave his only begotten Son, that whosoever believeth in him should not perish, but have everlasting life." (John 3:16)*

Love is an action word. So to answer the question, "Does God love us?" Yes, He Does! His action of giving his precious son, Jesus, so that we might have life more abundantly, has withstood the test of time.

Today's Prayer:
Lord, I just thank you for loving me despite where I have been.

Today's Reflection

What are some things that you have learned about the love and mind of God that you need to work on within yourself to be more Christ-like?

DAY 7
ENOUGH IS ENOUGH

"Go from the presence of a foolish man, when thou perceivest not in him the lips of knowledge."
Proverbs 14:7

Don't allow any situation to push you to the point that you say "Enough is Enough!" This is when a person gets to that mental stage when someone could get hurt or even killed because they have taken all that they can. If the situation seems to be headed down the pathway of you being fed up, then it's time to pull back and pump your brakes.

Walk away before you snap!

Sometimes it's best to walk away from a situation or relationship, not because you are giving up on it, but because if it continues the way it's going something detrimental could happen. I often say we never know what stress people are under and sometimes it's not the straw that breaks the camel's back...it's everything else that's already on the camel and the straw was the "Enough Is Enough."

Walk away before you snap! Sometimes a separation, divorce, breakup, quitting, agreeing to disagree .....isn't a bad option if it's going to prevent you from doing something you never thought you were capable of doing.

Today's Prayer:
Lord, please give me the strength to see relationships for what they are a walk away before it's too late.

Today's Reflection

What is the straw that has you at a point of saying enough is enough?

DAY 8
BLOOD VS WATER

If a man says, I love God, and hateth his brother, he is a liar: for he that loveth not his brother whom he hath seen, how can he love God whom he hath not seen?
1 John 4:20

There is an old proverb that says "Blood is Thicker than Water". This old proverb has often been interpreted to mean that the bonds of family (blood) will always be stronger than any friendship or relationship interest. Why is it so easy for some people to release, ditch, let go, or disown their relatives, siblings, or children, but will hold on to raggedy, sorry, no good, friends, boyfriends, girlfriends, mates, etc.?

> **Through the good, the bad, and the ugly family is still family.**

Understandably, everyone's family dynamic is different. In life, we meet different individuals that we forge covenant relationships because they have been there for us when the family has turned their back. In these types of situations, one would be quick to say that "Blood is NOT thicker than water."

Science has proven that the body doesn't completely die until the blood ceases to circulate. Through the good, the bad, and the ugly, family is still family. No matter what, you still have the same familial genes running through your blood. We are quick to forgive a friend who has hurt us but will hold a family member accountable for life for the same infraction. Unforgiveness is a set up to not live your life to the fullest. Have you ceased to live because you have cut off your blood supply for water?

Today's Prayer:
Lord, help me to forgive and keep my family strong.

Today's Reflection

Do you have any unforgiveness that you have been harboring?

DAY 9
LOVE VS UNCONDITIONAL LOVE

"This is my commandment, That ye love one another, as I have loved you."
John 15:12

Love is a very broad topic that can be difficult to define. Typically love is based upon a person's reasons or experiences.
1. The Agape love - which is the Godly love
2. The Philios love - which is the Brotherly love
3. The Eros love - which is the Erotic/ Passionate love
4. The Storge love – which is the Family Love

Love can be defined as having "Respect and High Regards for another person" plus a great attachment and dependency on a person, a caring and desire to help the person, and the desire for an exclusive intimate relationship with a person. Unconditional love has NO restrictions. This means you love someone regardless of their qualities, and without limitations; as in to love completely.

His love does not change.

Christ gave us the commandment to love one another as He has loved us. The love He has for us transcends all understanding. Regardless of what we have done or will do, His love does not change. When you say that you love someone, can you love them past and through their faults just as Christ does for us?

Today's Prayer:
Lord, help me to love others as you have loved me.

Today's Reflection
Are you loving others as Christ has loved you?

DAY 10
CO – PARENTING IN THE 21ST CENTURY

Train up a child in the way he should go: and when he is old, he will not depart from it.
Proverbs 22:6

It's NOT about you two as parents, but it's about how well you both can "Co-Parent in the 21st Century" to the point that you both can honor and respect each other when in the presence of the kid(s) and when the other parent isn't around. You speaking well of the other parent doesn't mean that you want them, but it shows your level of maturity. The respect or lack of respect from the kid(s) is a reflection of the training you have or haven't given them. If you allow them to be disrespectful to the other parent, it's not cute, but a reflection on YOU.

For those of you that "Co-Parent" & "Communicate" with the other Parent here are some important questions that could make a world of difference:

1. Do you say, "Thank you to the other parent and teach your child (ren) to say the same?"
2. Do you take credit for everything positive in the kid(s) lives because they live with you?
3. Is one of the reasons why you don't teach the kid(s) to honor and thank the other parent because you are harboring some negative emotions towards them?
4. Are you the parent that always feels that the other parent "Isn't Doing Enough"?
5. Have you moved on from what you and the other parent did or didn't have?

Today's Prayer:
Lord, help me to be the best parent I can be and train my child(ren) in the way that they should go.

Today's Reflection
What are some things you can do better as a parent?

James "J.R." Edwards

PART 2
YOU

DAY 11
IT'S TIME TO GROW UP

"There hath no temptation taken you but such as is common to man: but God is faithful, who will not suffer you to be tempted above that ye are able; but will with the temptation also make a way to escape, that ye may be able to bear it."
1 Corinthians 10:13

We all have a cross to bear. No cross, no crown! Various situations whether in the past or the present will illuminate the meaning of growing pains. Even while going through our growing pains we have to stand firmly on the living word and remind ourselves that He will never put more on us than we can bear. The pains we experience in life are all a part of our growth.

> **Your greatest victories ride upon the wings of your toughest battles.**

Growing pains are only immaturity being expelled out of our being. That's why before every promotion always comes accusations. Your greatest victories ride upon the wings of your toughest battles. The entire process is meant to build your faith and perfect your character. God already sees you at your expected end. So don't allow the pains of your past to punish your present and paralyze your future. You're growing pains are only growing you up; appreciate the process.

Today's Prayer:
Lord, thank you for giving me the grace and the mercy to grow into a better person.

Today's Reflection

What are some lessons you have learned from your growing pains?

DAY 12
DON'T CONFUSE DISCRETION WITH HYPOCRISY

"A prudent man foreseeth the evil, and hideth himself: but the simple pass on, and are punished."
Proverbs 22:3

Discretion is the quality of being careful about what you do and say so that people will not be embarrassed or offended, the quality of having or showing discernment or good judgment, and not likely to be seen or noticed by many people. Hypocrisy is the behavior of people who do things that they tell other people not to do, behavior that does not agree with what someone claims to believe or feel, and a person who claims or pretends to have certain beliefs about what is right but who behaves in a way that disagrees with those beliefs.

> **You are not supposed to tell all your business.**

Just because you are discreet doesn't mean that you are a hypocrite. You are not supposed to tell all your business. The same level of discretion that you have for your business you should have for others. Don't allow people to make you feel that your discretion is a form of you being hypocritical. Words of wisdom are written on discretion and hypocrisy and these can serve as foundational principles we use to govern our lives. In *Proverbs 2:11*, it is written, *"Discretion shall preserve thee, understanding shall keep thee."* It is also written in *Proverbs 11:9*, *"A hypocrite with his mouth destroyeth his neighbour: but through knowledge shall the just be delivered."* Ask yourself, are you discreet or are you a hypocrite?

Today's Prayer:
Lord, help me to be mindful of the words that come out of my mouth.

Today's Reflection

What are some things you have learned about yourself that you need to fix?

DAY 13
WHAT IS YOUR PRESENCE ENDORSING?

"And be not conformed to this world: but be ye transformed by the renewing of your mind, that ye may prove what is that good, and acceptable, and perfect, will of God."
Romans 12:2

We must be mindful of the people and things we decide to align ourselves with and endorse. Not all alignments are created equally. Some people want to align themselves with you because others trust the words that proceed out of your mouth and your mere presence can bring credibility.

> **Don't endorse someone else's agenda because you are trying to become known as a leader.**

Being a credible person attracts people who want to align themselves with you because your credibility is stronger than theirs, and they will use you to promote their agenda. Don't endorse someone else's agenda because you are trying to be known as a leader. It's unfortunate, but every hand that's on your back isn't congratulating you, it could be pushing you to an early demise. Let your works speak for you, and not your lips.

Today's Prayer:
Lord, give me the wisdom to continue to work on my credibility and align myself with the right people.

Today's Reflection

What are some alignments you need to remove yourself from?

DAY 14
EVERYTHING IS NOT FOR EVERYBODY

"For which cause we faint not; but though our outward man perish, yet the inward man is renewed day by day."
2 Corinthians 4:16

I know we live in a society that says "Keep it 100." Here's a suggestion, stop telling everybody about your struggles whether it be physically spiritually, mentally, or financially. Have you ever considered that the reason why some people hang on to what faith they do have in Christ, is because they don't see your struggles or know what's going on in your life? You can't share or testify about everything with and to everybody.

> **God will use your private hardships for a public ministry.**

Do you realize that some people think you got it going on? Consider this, the reason why people don't know you struggle in public is that you have been covered by the prayers you've made in secret. God is setting you up for something and you don't even know it. God will use your private hardships for a public ministry. Think about it and stop diminishing and killing your witness by telling too much too soon. When you consider the word enemy and you pronounce it slowly it begins to sound like you are saying inner me. I am convinced that the reason a lot of us aren't as effective as we could be is not as a result of the enemy, but it's a result of the inner me.

Today's Prayer:
Lord, help me to deal with my inner me.

Let Go of The Cookies

Today's Reflection
What are some "inner me" things you need to come to terms with?

DAY 15
DO YOU VALUE WHAT YOU HAVE?

"Judge not according to the appearance, but judge righteous judgment."
John 7:24

I awakened one morning thinking about an awesome church service. A man that would be looked at and labeled as a drunk came in off the streets during the midst of the praise, walked down to the altar, and laid there crying out to God. He had told one of the ministers before coming to the altar, "I Want What They Got!"

> **Don't take your gifts, talents, spouse, mate, family, friends, enemies, and definitely not God for granted.**

Here is food for thought: Is it possible that you have something good on the inside of you, or in your possession, and you don't even recognize its true value? Is it possible that others see what you possess and want what you have only because you don't appreciate what you have, or what you have has become common, familiar, and normal to you?

Don't take your gifts, talents, spouse, mate, family, friends, enemies, and definitely not God for granted, for they all play a significant role in your life, development, and purpose. Who or what have you lost sight of that might be of value to someone else? One man's trash is another man's treasure.

Today's Prayer:
Lord, help me to see and continue to see the value of the people and things in my life.

Today's Reflection
What are some things you have lost sight of the value of?

DAY 16
WHAT IS OBSTRUCTING YOUR VIEW

"(As it is written, I have made thee a father of many nations,) before him whom he believed, even God, who quickeneth the dead, and calleth those things which be not as though they were."
Romans 4:17

I love to travel and traveling via airplane allows me to see the world from a different vantage point. I noticed that as our altitude increased, the more beauty of the land I was able to see. It is something about seeing the landscape, trees, clouds, houses, etc. that is relaxing and satisfying. As we began to reach our destination and decrease altitude, the more mess I was able to see. There was trash on the streets, rundown buildings, and homes, etc. The things that I saw when the plane got lower were there all along when we were higher, but the difference was I wasn't close enough to see it.

> **When you change your altitude, you can change your outlook.**

Is it possible that the reason you can't see the beauty of your surroundings is that you are too close to the mess? When you change your altitude you can change your outlook. I often say *"Leadership can be hindered if leadership doesn't learn to distance itself from the crowd."* It's time to change your altitude.

Today's Prayer:
Lord, help me to still see the beauty of things through the mess.

Today's Reflection

What are some things you need to change your outlook on?

DAY 17
TIME FOR A CHANGE

"For there is hope of a tree, if it be cut down, that it will sprout again, and that the tender branch thereof will not cease."
Job 14:7

Whenever we talk about making a change in our life we or someone we know has said "*I am going to do a 360 in my life*". Then it changed to say, "*I am going to do a 180 in my life.*" If we use 360 to represent North and 180 to represent South, if we do a 360 we'll end up in the same direction we were headed, and if we do a 180, we will be entering back into what we were trying to get out of. So the only way to fully come out of something and to change directions is to do either a 90-degree turn or a 270 degree turn to go East or West.

> **Let's break familiarity because if #HeTurnedIt "For real", then you are not going to be hanging with the same people he delivered you from.**

Is it possible that the reason things look familiar to you is that when you changed, it was a 180-degree turn, which put you back in the direction you came out of? Then when you turned back around the scenery didn't change, only the cast members did?

Let's break familiarity because if #HeTurnedIt "For real", then you are not going to be hanging with the same people God delivered you from. Do a 180-degree turn to see where you've come from, do a 360-degree turn to see where you're headed, but do a 90 or 270-degree turn to change directions.

Today's Prayer:
Lord, guide me in my right direction to make effective changes in my life.

Today's Reflection
What are some things you are going to do differently?

DAY 18
SPECTATORS AND FANS

"And we know that the Son of God is come, and hath given us an understanding, that we may know him that is true, and we are in him that is true, even in his Son Jesus Christ. This is the true God, and eternal life."
1 John 5:20

Christology means the study of Christ and Christians, which means followers of Christ. Some people know of Christ, but they aren't supporters/followers of or have a relationship with Christ (Christians). As believers, we strive to not just be a follower, but also to have a relationship.

> **Some people just want to be viewed as being connected to you when they don't know you; they just know of you.**

Here's the illumination for your life. Some people just want to be viewed as being connected to you when they don't know you; they just know of you. They will do somewhat of a photobomb or photoshop into your life which gives others the thought or impression that you are in a relationship with them, so when they speak of you it makes their words appear to carry weight.

There are two types of people in our lives, we have spectators and fans, A spectator is a person who looks on or watches, an onlooker, or an observer. A fan is an enthusiastic devotee, follower, supporter, or admirer of. Fans will pray for you, but spectators will prey on you. It's important to know and accept the roles of the people in your life.

Today's Prayer:
Lord, give me an understanding of the roles people have in my life.

Today's Reflection
What roles do the people in your life carry?

DAY 19
YOU ARE VALUABLE

"I will praise thee; for I am fearfully and wonderfully made: marvelous are thy works; and that my soul knoweth right well."
Psalm 139:14

To the wrong person, you will never have worth. You will never meet up to their expectations, but to the right person, you will mean everything. The most important person that needs to know your value and self-worth is you. Don't allow anyone or any situation to diminish your value and your self-worth.

> **You are valuable because you are a direct reflection of God's splendor and greatness among all humanity.**

8 tips to help you start valuing yourself:
1. Make Jesus your priority and not a secondary option.
2. Don't allow other people's lack of planning to become your emergency.
3. Write your vision lucidly and read over it daily to maintain focus on the goals you want to achieve.
4. Stop sharing your visions with myopic friends & family.
5. Keep negative thinkers and talkers out of your ears.
6. Pray that your "will" lines up with God's "will" for your life.
7. Follow through and don't be afraid of making adjustments along the way.
8. Enjoy the journey, celebrate every moment, and encourage yourself daily.

I declare unto you that you are valuable because you are a direct reflection of God's splendor and greatness among all humanity.

Today's Prayer:
Lord, help me to show myself the love that I deserve.

Today's Reflection
What things do you need to put in place to increase your self-love?

DAY 20
DO YOU SEE WHAT THEY SEE IN YOU?
"And the Lord said, Simon, Simon, behold, Satan hath desired to have you, that he may sift you as wheat:"
Luke 22:31

The enemy doesn't fight against those whom he already has. It's only those that are a threat to his kingdom that he desires to sift like wheat. Is it possible that the reason you are being fought so hard and struggle so much is that your adversaries see more in you than you see and accredit to yourself? Is there a possible assignment on your life for you to carry out, but you are holding on to dead weight instead of allowing your gift to be stirred up?

Your gift is closely related to the assignment.

That is why when you do good, evil is always present. Your gift is closely related to your assignment. When you discover your gift, it can lead to your assignment and your assignment will lead you to your purpose; thus landing you in your destiny. It is a process.

Consider the life of Joseph in the book of Genesis. He had a dream and sharing that dream led to his first assignment of getting thrown in the pit. Joseph's pit experience is what connected him to his destiny. Just because you don't see it doesn't mean that it is not there.

Today's Prayer:
Lord, help me to see and understand the gifts on the inside of me so I can walk into my destiny.

Today's Reflection
What are the gifts that you need to acknowledge?

James "J.R." Edwards

PART 3
THE PLAN

DAY 21
ARE YOU FOLLOWING THE PLAN?

"And let us not be weary in well doing: for in due season we shall reap if we faint not."
Galatians 6:9

Change does not happen overnight, so don't be discouraged by the way things are looking right now. Stay the course and follow the plan that has been designed for your life. In *Jerimiah 29:11*, it is written, *"For I know the thoughts that I think toward you, saith the Lord, thoughts of peace, and not of evil, to give you an expected end."* God is shaping our character with every life experience we encounter.

A plan in place is ideas put into practice.

Interwoven between the fabrics of success, threads a plan. If you desire better health holistically (spiritual, mental, and physical), you have to plan and implement healthier lifestyle changes: daily devotional studies, avoid negativity and exercise routinely. A plan in place is ideas put into practice. Daily you must continue to grow, exercise your faith, and work on your ideas.

There will be moments where it seems like those around you are rapidly getting ahead of you, but remain focused. Do not allow the advancements of others to cause you to move outside of or faster than your plan calls for. Take your time and follow the plan and watch it comes to pass.

Today's Prayer:
Father, please grant me the patience, strategy, and tenacity to fulfill the plan that you have for my life.

Today's Reflection
What is the plan God has for your life?

DAY 22
WHAT DO YOU DO WHEN YOUR PROMISE DIES?

"Trust in the Lord with all your heart, and lean not unto your understanding. In all your ways acknowledge him, and he shall direct your paths."
Proverbs 3:5-6

Have you ever been given a promise that was full of life, but once the promise seems to be coming to pass it ends up dying? Take a moment to recall to your mind that promise. Was it a promise of life for a loved one that ended up dying? Was it a dream, a goal, a business venture, or a relationship that died? How did you deal with it or are you still dealing with it now?

> **Trust in the only man that can perform a resurrection.**

The death of someone or something is one of the toughest realities to cope with because it leaves us with so many questions as to why it had to happen at a particular moment in life. One other reason that makes death so hard to deal with is we never really get an answer to the question of why.

When it seems that your promise has died, still trust him. Why? In John 11:25-26 it is written, *"Jesus said unto her, I am the resurrection, and the life: he that believeth in me, though he were dead, yet shall he live:" And whosoever liveth and believeth in me shall never die. Believest thou this?"* Why not trust in the only man that can perform a resurrection to a seemingly dead promise or situation?

Today's Prayer:
Lord, I trust you and I will not lean to my understanding as you guide me.

Today's Reflection

What are the promises you are trusting and believing God to be resurrected?

DAY 23
WHAT IS THE CAUSE FOR YOUR CURRENT STORM?

"These things I have spoken unto you, that in me ye might have peace. In the world ye shall have tribulation: but be of good cheer; I have overcome the world."
John 16:33

We have all encountered the storms of life. I submit to you that there are 3 types of storms we could face.

1. A storm because of your disobedience like that of Jonah (Jonah chapter 1)
2. A storm because of others like that of Apostle Paul being shipwrecked (Acts chapter 27)
3. A storm of obedience like that of the disciples doing as Jesus had told them to do (Matthew 14:20, Luke 8:22)

> **God allows for the various storms to come our way to increase our faith.**

Regardless of the storm, you have encountered, there is one common denominator. That common denominator is you. We have to remember that God allows for the various storms to come our way to increase our faith. We all have probably heard this idiom or one similar to it. "We all have encountered a storm..... either we are entering a storm, coming out a storm, or amid a storm." How are you handling your storm?

Today's Prayer:
Lord, help me to learn the lessons of my storms.

Today's Reflection

What kind is/was yours: because of your disobedience, because of others, or because of your obedience?

DAY 24
NAVIGATING THROUGH THE TEST

"My brethren, count it all joy when ye fall into divers temptations; Knowing this, that the trying of your faith worketh patience."
James 1:3

We can find ourselves ready to respond to the calamity that is unfolding right before our eyes. When you see all of the trials coming your way, take a moment to step back and consider its purpose. Oftentimes, we do not see the purpose until we have come out.

> **No matter what happens or what is said, don't stop moving.**

The test of your growth, maturity, and wisdom can be measured by how well you respond. Only a fool will disclose all that they know, but a wise person will hold what they know and use it as fuel for the journey. Stop worrying about what people have to say about you. Things will come up to attempt to impede your progress in fulfilling the plan God has for your life. No matter what happens or what is said, don't stop moving. So as long as there is breathe in your body keep pushing and pressing.

Today's Prayer:
Lord, give me the strength to withstand the trials that come my way and keep moving.

Let Go of The Cookies

Today's Reflection

What are the things you need to quit worrying about so you can continue to move forward?

DAY 25
TIME, SEASON, AND PURPOSE

"To everything, there is a season, and a time to every purpose under the heaven:"
Ecclesiastes 3:1

What is Time? What is Season? What is Purpose?
- Time tells us when to do what we're going to do and how long we have to get it done.
- The season deals with a specific time in which we are to sow or to plant. Our season tells us what kind of seeds we should be sowing when the time is right.
- Purpose deals with the time we should be reaping the harvest from what we have sown in our proper season.

> **A farmer doesn't reap corn in his season, but a farmer reaps corn when it's harvest time.**

What time is it for you? Are you in your season or are you in your purpose and how do you know? Is it possible that the reason you haven't seen a harvest is that you are trying to reap when you should be sowing? There are a time and season for everything. Write your plan out in the order that it should go, so you can visualize the result. A farmer doesn't reap corn in his season, but a farmer reaps corn when it's harvest time. Where are you at this moment in your life?

Today's Prayer:
Lord, give me insight into this moment in my life so that I can move forward.

Today's Reflection

Where are you in the season of your life? Do you need to make any changes?

DAY 26
PEACE

When a man's ways please the Lord, he makes even his enemies be at peace with him.
Proverbs 16:7

God has granted you peace during this time and season you are in right now. There is nothing like the peace that God bestows upon us. You are surrounded by so much peace that nothing can touch you. It is written by the Apostle Paul in *Philippians 3:14, "I press toward the mark for the prize of the high calling of God in Christ Jesus."* No matter what you do, keep pushing and pressing.

> **God is preparing a table before you in the presence of your enemies**

Your enemies haven't seen anything yet. *"But as it is written, Eye hath not seen, nor ear heard, neither have entered into the heart of man, the things which God hath prepared for them that love him." 1 Corinthians 2:9.* God is preparing a table before you in the presence of your enemies; since it's a prepared table by God, you might as well go ahead, eat, and enjoy the meal. Don't delete your enemies yet, and don't deactivate your social media accounts either, because they're on the guest list.

Today's Prayer:
Lord, thank you for the peace you have given me in this season of my life.

Today's Reflection

Are there some things you need to let go of to fully walk in the peace God has given you?

DAY 27
IT'S NOT DEAD, IT'S ONLY ASLEEP

When Jesus heard that, he said, This sickness is not unto death, but for the glory of God, that the Son of God might be glorified thereby.
John 11:11

Don't give up right now, you are too close to your awakening. You may feel that your dreams and goals are dead, but they are not, they are only asleep. Sometimes God will permit the temporary death of something so that the glory of God can be revealed by a resurrection. Read the story of the resurrection of Lazarus of Bethany in the book of John chapter 11. It lays out the resurrecting power of Jesus.

> **What you thought was dead is about to be awakened from its sleep.**

Be encouraged by my brother or sister that, your temporary setback does not mean permanent defeat. What you thought was dead is about to be awakened from its sleep. Our timing is not God's timing. We have to learn to be patient and to trust the process. The process is what creates the lessons learned and the building of your faith. Then you will discover that this was a "must need to go through the situation." Watch how God will move on your behalf when the time is right.

Today's Prayer:
Lord, strengthen me to trust the process as I go through my "must need to go through the situation."

Today's Reflection

What some ideas, goals, and dreams you think are dead or that you have seen die?

DAY 28
CHOOSE TO BE OPTIMISTIC

Let no corrupt communication proceed out of your mouth, but that which is good to the use of edifying, that it may minister grace unto the hearers."
Ephesians 4:29

A pessimist tends to see the negative in everything. Pessimistic people will always:
- See the 'lie' in believe
- The 'over' in 'lover'
- The "end" in friends
- The "rust" in trust
- The "if" in life.

> **Don't allow the inevitable things that accompany life's journey to rob or steal your optimistic view on life and living.**

We have to make a conscious decision to be positive and hopeful about the future. That is what being optimistic is all about. Don't allow the inevitable things that accompany life's journey to rob or steal your optimistic view on life and living. Just as the word 'lie' was only used to construct the word believe; it is within your life, and the various obstacles you've faced up to this point. Those obstacles were only put there to form and construct you into someone greater than who and what you already are. Make your choice and stick to it.

Today's Prayer:
Lord, change my view to be more positive towards the thing that comes to me in my life.

Today's Reflection

What are the pessimistic viewpoints you need to get rid of?

DAY 29
MONEY

Now he that ministereth seed to the sower both minister bread for your food, and multiply your seed sown, and increase the fruits of your righteousness;)"
2 Corinthians 9:10

Money is more than what you have in the bank. Money serves as a medium of exchange to what is accepted as a means of payment for products, goods, services, etc. You are earning it, but are you keeping it? What lifestyle will make you comfortable enough that you are willing to stop upgrading it every time you earn more?

> **If you upgrade your lifestyle every time you receive an increase, you will never see your financial growth.**

What you do with your money after you receive it has a direct impact on your future. We have to be consistent in sowing seed and be mindful of the ground we put it in. If you upgrade your lifestyle every time you receive an increase, you will never see your financial growth. Choose your lifestyle, but also gradually allow your income to have a long-distance relationship with your Debt to Income Ratio until you can become #DebtFree. It's not about how much one can earn, but it's about how much one can keep. Making sound decisions allows us to be in a position to establish a legacy for our children's children.

Today's Prayer:
Lord, give me the wisdom to make better financial decisions.

Today's Reflection

What are the things you need to let go of to be more financially sound?

DAY 30
IT'S STILL GOING TO COME TO PASS

And Joshua said unto the people, Sanctify yourselves: for tomorrow the Lord will do wonders among you.
Joshua 3:5

We all have had many prophecies or words that were spoken over our lives that we may have forgotten or may even be some that you thought were not going to come to pass. You must remember that it is written, *"God is not a man, that he should lie; neither the son of man, that he should repent: hath he said, and shall he not do it? or hath he spoken, and shall he not make it good?" Numbers 23:19.*

> **You have to continue to keep Jesus first in your life.**

Have faith and trust him and know that the words that have been spoken over our lives will come to pass. If He said it, he will bring it to pass. You will see that in this year the seed shall come to pass and manifest itself in your life, DOUBLE. You have to continue to keep Jesus first in your life. You had to experience the past to appreciate what is about to take place in your future.

Today's Prayer:
Lord, I just thank you for this journey and I am open and ready to receive what you have placed before me.

Today's Reflection

What are things that you are letting go to make room to receive?

James "J.R." Edwards

www.ingramcontent.com/pod-product-compliance
Lightning Source LLC
Chambersburg PA
CBHW071839290426
44109CB00017B/1863